A PRACTICAL METHOD

FOR *VIOLIN*

By

NICOLAS LAOUREUX

Adopted by the Conservatories of Brussels, Amsterdam, The Hague, Glasgow
Cologne, Aix-la-Chapelle, and the principal Academies of Belgium, Holland,
Rhenish Prussia, France, South America, etc.

Translated from the Third French Edition by
Dr. TH. BAKER

IN FOUR PARTS

PART I: Elements of Bowing and Left-Hand Technique

PART I (Supplement): Thirty Progressive Studies in the First Position
     preceded by Preparatory Exercises

PART II: The Five Positions, and Their Employment—Practical Study
     of the Démanché

PART II (Supplement): Twenty-Eight Progressive Studies preceded by
     Preparatory Exercises

PARTS I and II, in One Volume (Without Supplements)

PART III: School of Bowing—Preparatory Studies to the Kreutzer, Fiorillo
     and Rode Studies

PART IV: Virtuosity of the Left Hand—Exercises in the Form of Legato
     Scales, Arpeggios, Double-Stops, etc.

ED-1451

ISBN 978-0-7935-5454-6

G. SCHIRMER, *Inc.*

DISTRIBUTED BY

7777 W. BLUEMOUND RD. P.O. BOX 13819 MILWAUKEE, WI 53213

Practical Method for the Violin

BY NICOLAS LAOUREUX

PART II
The Positions

Violin "methods" generally pass from the first position to the second, from the second to the third, and so on in numerical order.

To go directly from the first to the third position seems simpler and easier. Later, the pupil will find his second position between the first and the third. Moreover, this manner of proceeding will allow us to begin, at the same time, the highly important study of the shifts. To learn the fingerings of the positions seems, at first, to be the difficult point. Yet this is only a matter of memorizing figures.

Take a pupil who already knows his positions, and give him a fairly rapid slurred passage going from one position to another. The difficulty which he will encounter in playing it will be precisely in the changes of position which we call "shifts."

To forestall this difficulty at the outset by numerous exercises in shifting, is absolutely indispensable It is important, in order to shift easily, that the pupil should hold the palm of the hand well away from the neck of the instrument, and especially avoid resting the hand against the edge of the violin when arriving at the third position. The thumb should not be bent round the bottom of the neck. This would cause a displacement of the position of the hand, and would later render the shift from the third to the fifth position very awkward.

In both the 1st and 3d positions keep the thumb opposite the first finger

Scale of C major in the 3d Position

Preparation

1

2

22693

Étude in the 3ª Position

Grand détaché
Moderato

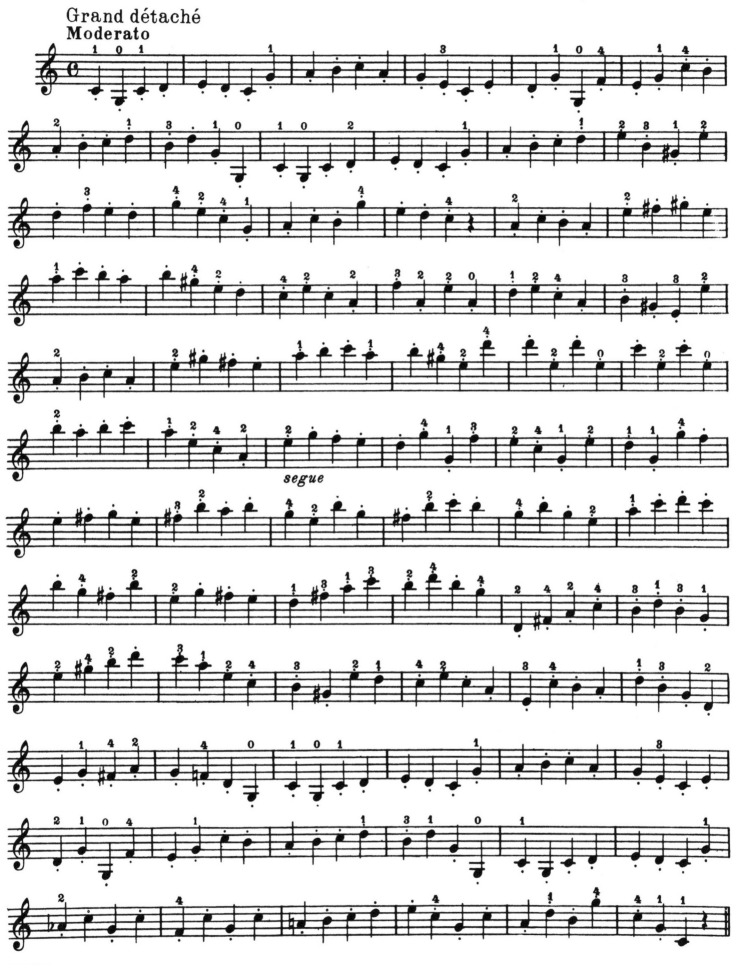

segue

Exercise in the 3ᵈ Position

Use the whole bow, the fingers striking firmly.

Moderato

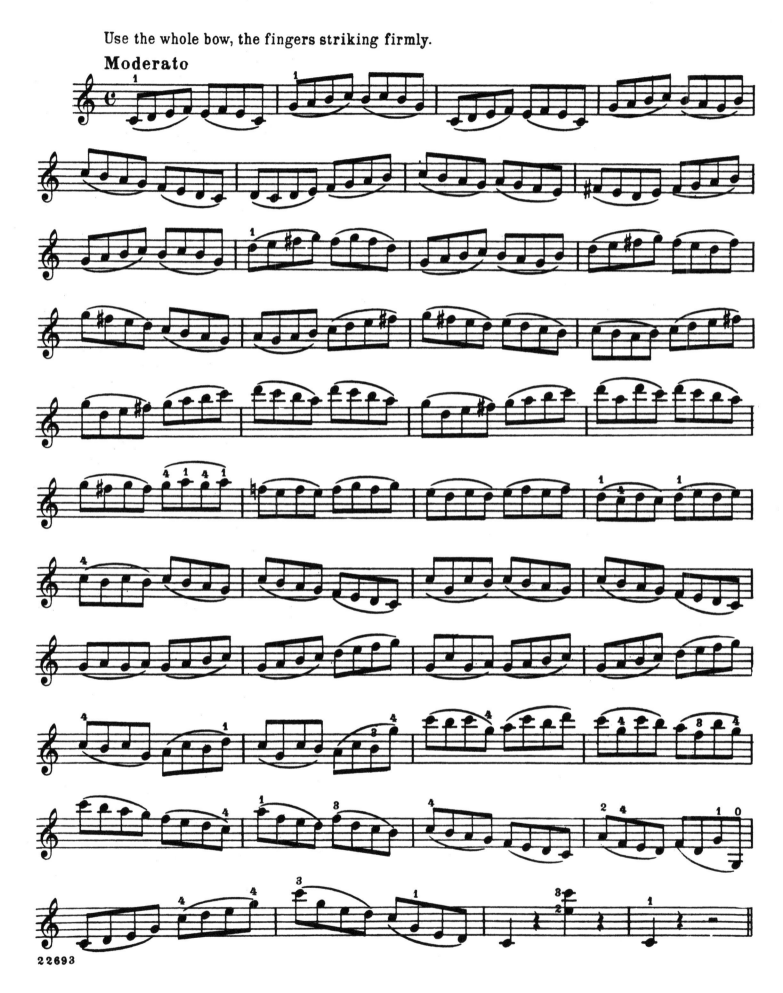

Exercise in Going from the 1st to the 3d Position

Shift with the open string. The thumb opposite the first finger. When shifting, let the hand slide lightly without pressing the neck.

ÉTUDE

1st and 3d Positions
Andante

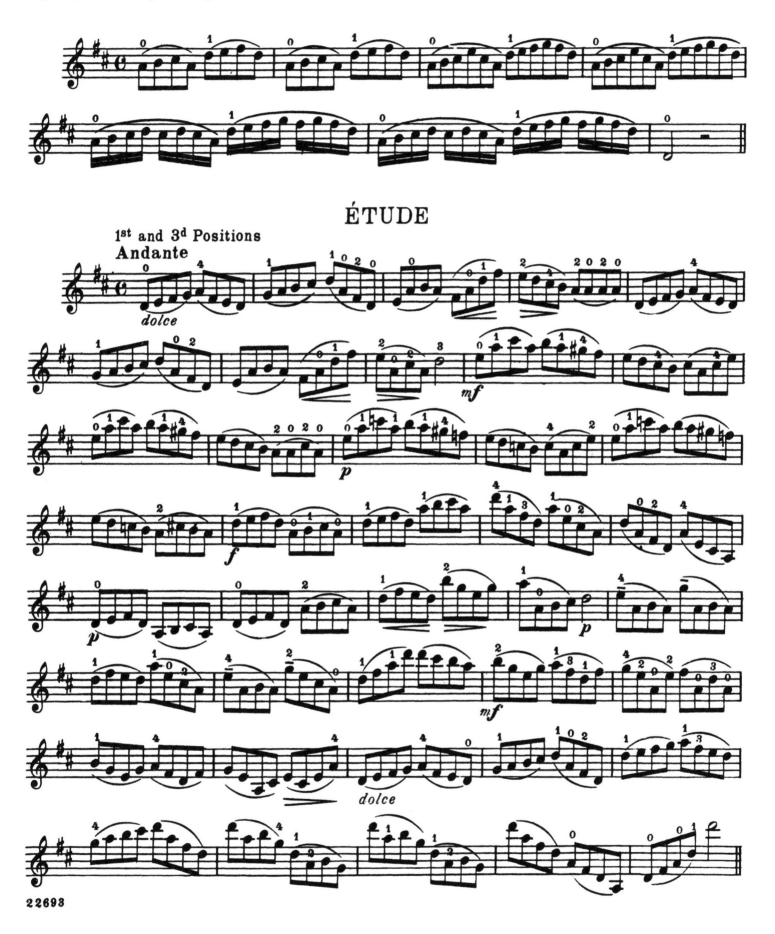

The pupil will have to practise the following exercises until the passage from the 1st to the 3d position becomes quite easy with any finger.

Changing the Position with Two Different Fingers

Example

The portamento must start from the first note, i.e., the finger of that note must reach the higher position before the one of the second note touches the string.

Example

The teacher will perceive that the small note is meant only to indicate the movement of the finger which operates the change of position; analyzing the exercise as below, the pupil will see the utility of this system for obtaining a proper portamento.

N.B. The small note should not be heard.

Play each measure 4 times.

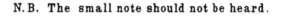

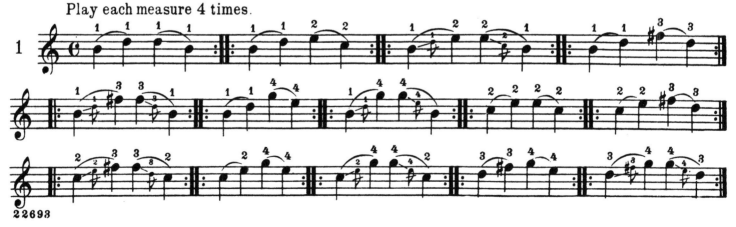

Keep the 1st finger on the string.

8

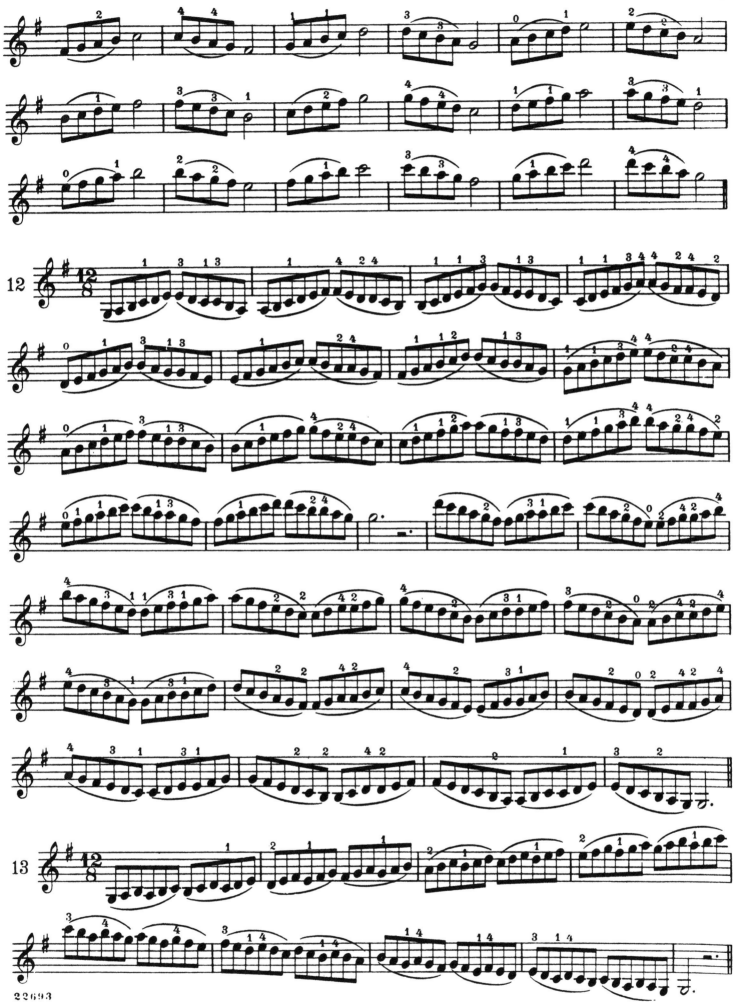

MELODIE
Exercise in Shifting

The shifting finger must move so rapidly that the slide from one note to the other is inaudible.

ÉTUDE
1st and 3d Positions

Moderato, largamente

Extension of the 4th Finger in the 3d Position (Harmonics)

By extending the 4th finger in the 3d position one can get the harmonic tone an octave higher than the open string. It is marked $\frac{4}{0}$, which indicates that the finger must only lightly touch the string, without pressing it.

N. B. To let the harmonic sound, the other fingers must not touch the string.

Example

The harmonic may also be reached by starting with the 4th finger from the 1st position. Let the hand slide gently from 1st to 3d position, while slightly raising and extending the 4th finger.

ÉTUDE

22693

On the 2ᵈ Position, lying between the 1ˢᵗ and 3ᵈ

The preceding exercises in passing from the 1ˢᵗ to the 3ᵈ position, having given the pupil sufficient practice in shifting, it is well now to introduce the 2ᵈ position by progressive exercises. This manner of proceeding will have the advantage of showing the pupil in what cases that position is used; moreover, it will make it easier to reach, as similar or corresponding passages, with the same fingerings for the corresponding notes, are given in the 1ˢᵗ, 2ᵈ and 3ᵈ positions.

* For the sake of brevity, the position will hereafter be indicated by a simple Roman numeral (I, II, III, etc.)

22693

Scale of G major in the 2d Position

Scale of C major in the 2d Position

Keep the first and fourth fingers on the strings as long as possible.

ÉTUDE
1st, 2d and 3d Positions

ETUDE

(1) Two bows to each measure, very slowly.

ÉTUDE

To be practised at first with broad detached strokes, from middle to point.

Moderato

The Octave

Preparatory Exercises

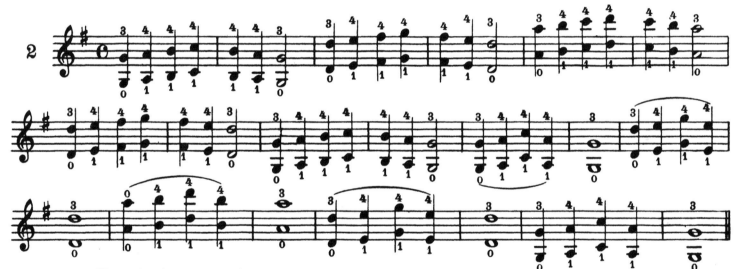

Keep the fingers on the strings.

ÉTUDE

N.B. Keep the 1st and 4th fingers down; lift them only to change fingerings or strings.

Same Exercise with Grand détaché

DOUBLE-STOPPING

The pupil finds difficulty in distinguishing between major and minor intervals. Besides the fact that his ear is not trained to recognize two tones at once, he has no exact idea how near together or far apart are the tones forming these two intervals. In order to render the work clearer and easier we shall begin with broken intervals.

The Sixth, starting from the Octave

Without lifting the finger to pass from one octave to another.

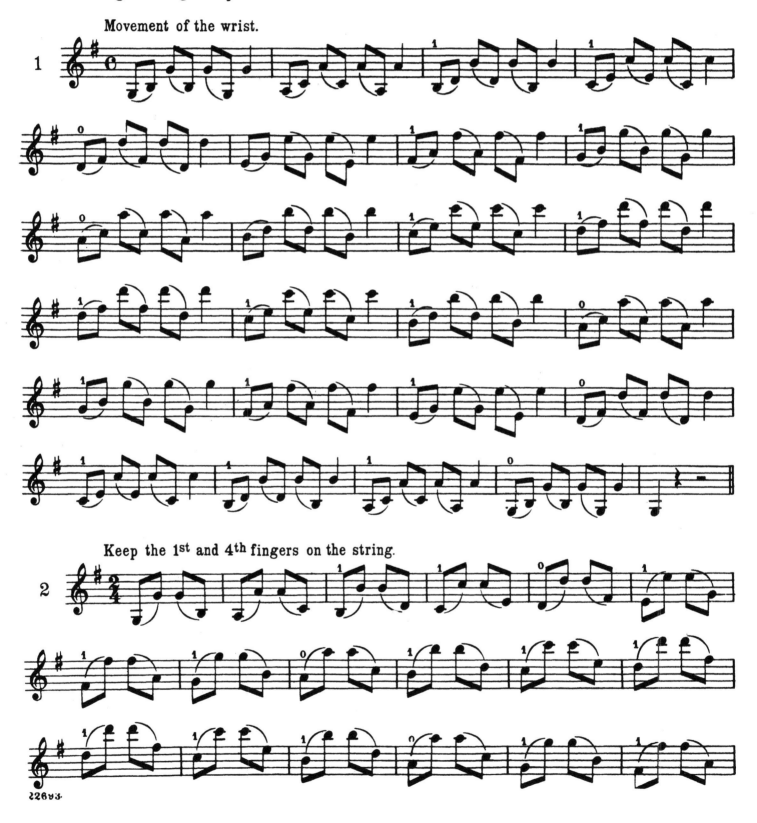

28

In playing sixths, the interval of separation between the fingers is either one or two half-steps, according to the key; in thirds the interval of separation (not of pitch) of the fingers is either three or four half-steps. In order that the pupil may not be in doubt when he has to play two notes at one time, we shall employ the following graphic signs: ⌐ indicates, in sixths, that the fingers are two half-steps apart; in thirds, that they are four half-steps apart;] indicates, in sixths, that the fingers are one half-step apart; in thirds, that they are three half-steps apart. To sum up, in either sixths or thirds, ⌐ indicates the larger interval of separation between the fingers.

Octaves, Sevenths, Sixths

Keep down the fingers which take the **octave**.

Octaves, Seconds, Thirds and Fifths

Set the 1st finger squarely upon the fifth at the beginning of the measure.

A Special Study on Thirds

ÉTUDE

N.B. This study serves as a preparation to the following one in double-stops. The pupil will have to keep the first finger on the string throughout each measure; and the others, after being placed on the strings, must remain till the end of the measure.

Staccato secco

22693

ÉTUDE

Review of the Double-stops
Andante

ÉTUDE

The Détaché. With the whole bow, separating the notes.

Moderato

22693

TRILLS

Their Divisions and Endings

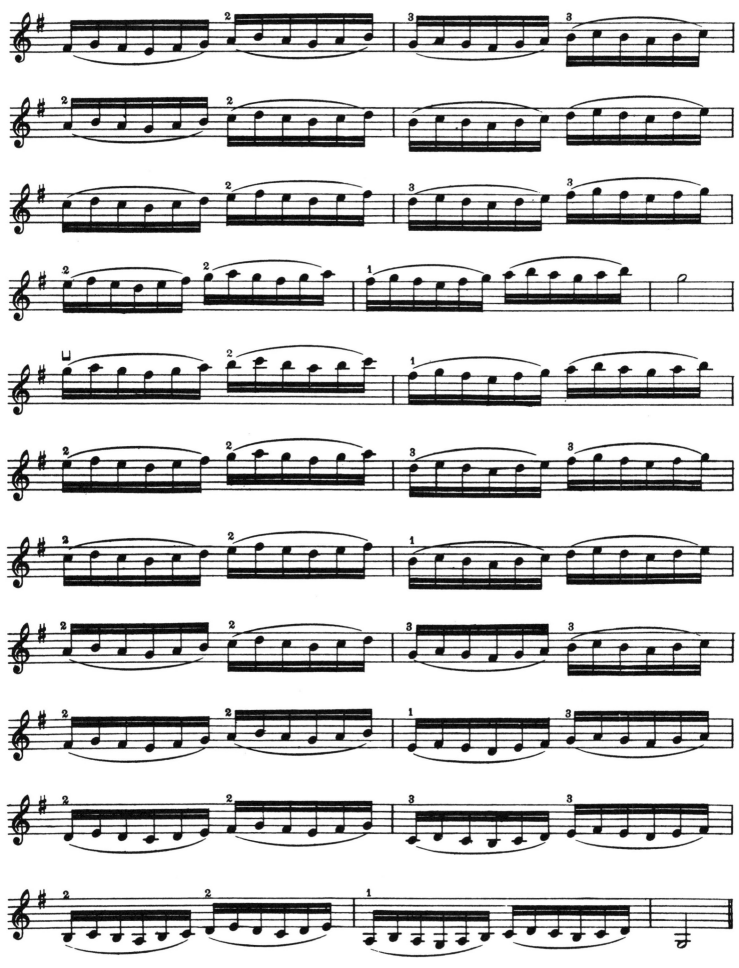

Lento

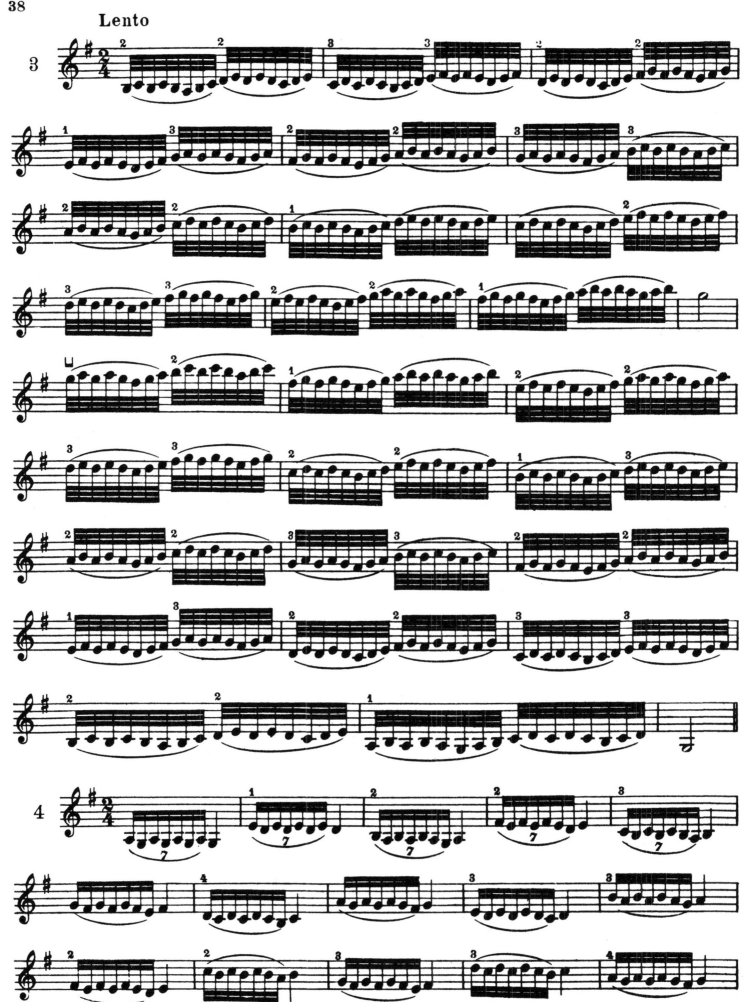

PREPARED TRILLS

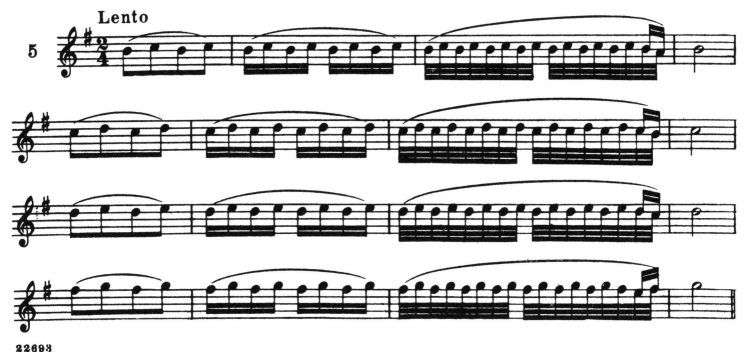

Beginning the trills slowly, as in the preceding exercises.

STUDY OF VARIOUS TRILLS

THE 4th AND 5th POSITIONS

In order to pass easily from the first to the fourth and fifth positions, the pupil will have to bring the hand well away from the neck, and hold the neck between the first joint of the thumb and the third joint of the first finger, so that he need not alter the position of the hand, and will have the same freedom in moving and placing his fingers in the fourth and fifth positions, as in the first.

Scale in D major: 4th position

Scale in E major: 4th position

44

6

In shifting to the higher positions the thumb must move an equal distance with the hand until the thumb reaches the curve of the neck where the latter joins the body of the violin. This is about at the fourth position.

1

4

5

6

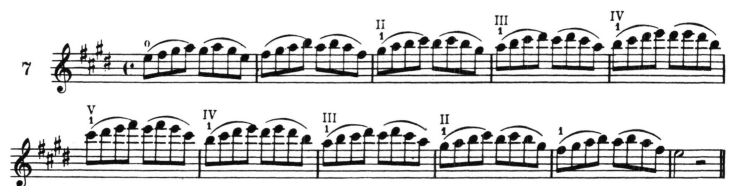

7

Octaves, in All Five Positions

1

48

Study in Octaves in the Five Positions

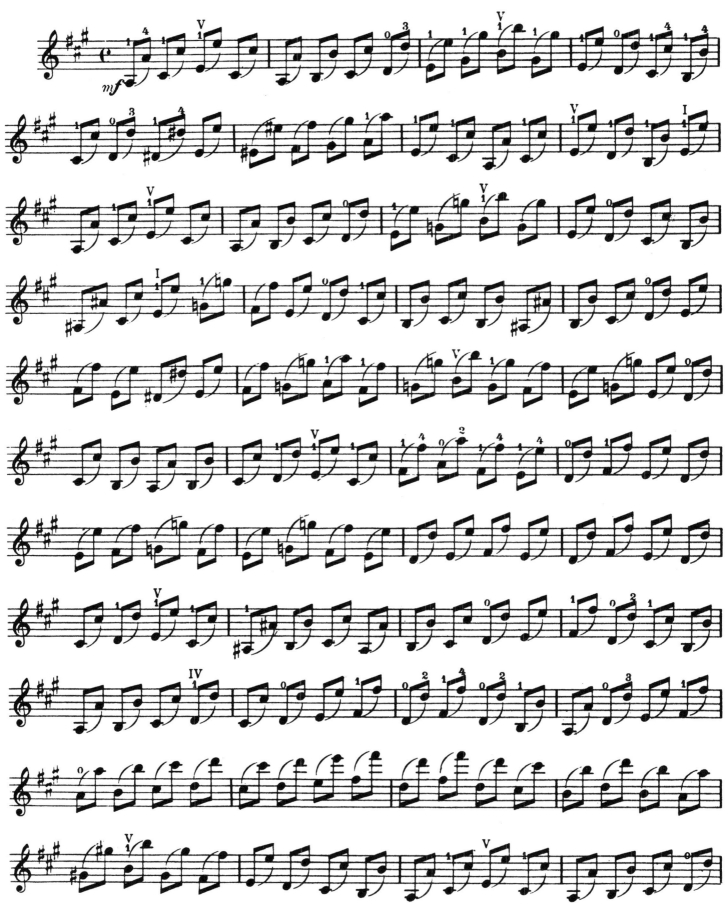

22693

Exercise in the 5th position

Exercises requiring the same fingering in the five positions

1

2   2d position

Study in the Five Positions

Moderato-Sostenuto

Exercise in the Five Positions

1

2 2d position

3 3d position

51

22693

ÉTUDE ON THE MARTELÉ

STUDY IN THE FIVE POSITIONS

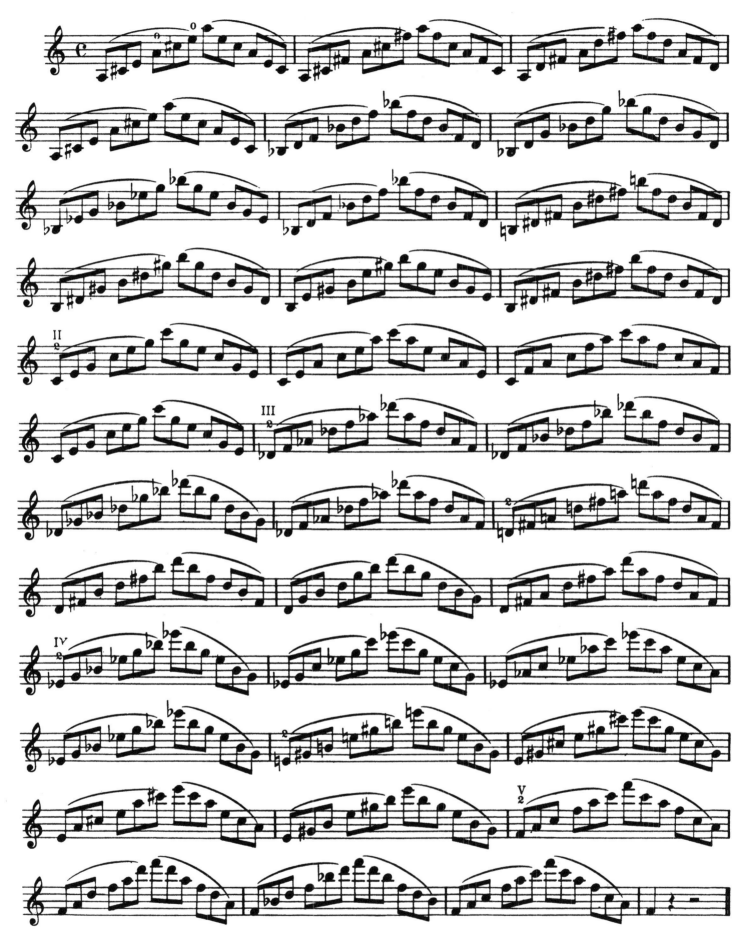

STUDY IN THE FIVE POSITIONS

ETUDE